YELLOWSTONE
National Park

by Tom Streissguth

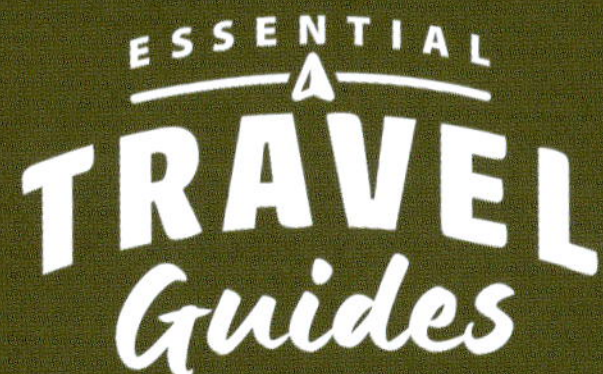

Essential Library
An Imprint of Abdo Publishing
abdobooks.com

ABDOBOOKS.COM

Published by Abdo Publishing, a division of ABDO, PO Box 398166, Minneapolis, Minnesota 55439.

Printed in China.
052025
092025

Cover Photo: Shutterstock Images
Interior Photos: William Henry Jackson/Denver Photographic Library/USGS, 4–5; William Henry Jackson/National Park Service/USGS, 7; Geoffrey Clements/VCG/Corbis Historical/Getty Images, 11; Library of Congress/VCG/Corbis Historical/Getty Images, 13; Shutterstock Images, 14, 19, 48, 50, 69, 85; Kit Leong/Shutterstock Images, 16–17, 92; wanderluster/E+/Getty Images, 21; NPS Photo/Alamy, 22; George Rose/Getty Images News/Getty Images, 25; Allan Hartley/Alamy, 26; Zack Frank/Shutterstock Images, 28–29; Thomas Trompeter/Shutterstock Images, 32; Janson George/Shutterstock Images, 33; Jonathan Newton/Getty Images News/Getty Images, 35, 75, 98; Alan Majchrowicz/Photodisc/Getty Images, 36; Tami Freed/Shutterstock Images, 39; Cheri Alguire/Shutterstock Images, 40; Andriy Blokhin/Alamy, 42–43; Michael Gordon/Shutterstock Images, 45; William Campbell/Corbis News/Getty Images, 52–53; Alexander Gardner/Archive Photos/Getty Images, 54; George Ostertag/Alamy, 57; Jim Peaco/National Park Service, 60; Duncan Selby/Alamy, 62; William Campbell/Getty Images News/Getty Images, 64–65; Wolfgang Kaehler/Avalon/Universal Images Group/Getty Images, 66; Michelle Holihan/Shutterstock Images, 72; Maciej Bledowski/Shutterstock Images, 76; Hanjo Hellmann/Alamy, 78–79; Jeffrey B. Ross/Shutterstock Images, 82; Robert Way/Shutterstock Images, 86; Chon Kit Leong/Alamy, 88–89; Andrew Sabai/Alamy, 91; ABC Collection/Alamy, 97; Red Line Editorial, 101

Editor: Laura Stickney
Series Designer: Joshua Olson

Library of Congress Control Number: 2024948599

PUBLISHER'S CATALOGING-IN-PUBLICATION DATA

Names: Streissguth, Tom, author.
Title: Yellowstone National Park / by Tom Streissguth
Description: Minneapolis, Minnesota: Abdo Publishing, 2026 | Series: Essential travel guides | Includes online resources and index.
Identifiers: ISBN 9781098297138 (lib. bdg.) | ISBN 9798384919650 (ebook)
Subjects: LCSH: Yellowstone National Park--Juvenile literature. | Travel--Juvenile literature. | United States--Guidebooks--Juvenile literature. | National parks and reserves--Juvenile literature. | Historic sites--Juvenile literature.
Classification: DDC 917.8752--dc23

CONTENTS

CHAPTER
ONE

THE HISTORY OF YELLOWSTONE NATIONAL PARK

The Yellowstone region in what is now the western United States has a long history. It has been known to American Indian groups for thousands of years. In the 1800s, the Crow, Shoshone, and Lakota peoples ventured into the territory to hunt deer, elk, bears, and antelope. They also collected obsidian from the area. This hard, dark volcanic rock could be shaped into sharp cutting tools and arrowheads.

American Indian peoples crossed trails in the Yellowstone region on their way to the Great Plains, where they followed bison herds north or south according to the season. There were many legends and rites linked to Yellowstone's geysers and hot thermal springs. The Kiowa people traced their origins to a cauldron of hot mud that

Geologist Ferdinand Hayden, *seated in center*, was photographed in 1870 with members of the Hayden expedition. The team included artists, zoologists, naturalists, and other experts.

bubbled from a dark cave near Yellowstone Lake. Years later, this mud spring was named the Dragon's Mouth.

Exploring the West

While American Indians had long been familiar with the Yellowstone region, most white settlers in the 1800s saw it as a distant, sparsely populated territory. Since the end of the American Civil War (1861–1865), the US Congress had been sending teams of explorers to survey the western United States. Government officials wanted to map the territories there, which would eventually become US states. They wanted information on resources such as land, water, soil, animals, and minerals. Another important goal of the expeditions was to find good locations for future roads, railways, and forts.

Discovering Yellowstone

Several expeditions visited Yellowstone in the 1800s. The 1869 Folsom–Cook expedition and the 1870 Washburn–Doane expedition traveled through the region. The 1869 group discovered Tower Fall, Mud Volcano, West Thumb, Shoshone Lake, and the Firehole River geyser basin. The 1870 group gave the Old Faithful geyser its name. The group also explored the Grand Canyon of the Yellowstone, a deep gorge in which the Yellowstone River tumbles over a series of waterfalls. Expedition member Gustavus Doane described the canyon in a report. He wrote, "Standing on the brink of the chasm the heavy roaring of the imprisoned river comes to the ear in a sort of hollow, hungry growl. . . . It is grand, gloomy, and terrible."[1]

The Tukudika band of Shoshone lived and hunted in parts of what are now northwestern Wyoming, southwestern Montana, and eastern Idaho for thousands of years. William Jackson photographed a Tukudika family in 1871.

The US Army relied on these roads and forts in its campaigns against American Indians, who had been living in and around the Rocky Mountains for thousands of years. The army's mission was to force American Indian nations, including the Shoshone, Nimiipuu (Nez Perce), Blackfoot, and Lakota, onto reservations. US leaders believed this would make the settlement of western territories and the establishment of new states easier.

Before the 1870s, only a few mountaineers and trappers—who hunted animals for their valuable pelts—had seen the Yellowstone region. They told tales of a strange land with spouting geysers, hot pools, and vents that gave off towers of steam. Some people thought these descriptions were nothing more than tall tales.

Explorer John Colter may have ventured into the area during the winter of 1807–1808. But neither he nor others had left a written record of the Yellowstone region. To many people in the United States, the area remained a mystery.

In 1870, Congress voted to finance four western expeditions.[2] One would be an exploration of the headwaters of the Yellowstone River in the territory of Wyoming, led by geologist and explorer Ferdinand Hayden. Congress granted the expedition a budget of $40,000.[3] This is equal to about $957,300 in 2024.[4]

To find his way through the wilderness, Hayden would need experienced guides. He hired horse and mule drivers along with scientists, mapmakers, geologists, and surveyors. He also needed more than just scientific reports to bring back to Congress. Words were important, but pictures were more effective. He would have to find some way to illustrate the descriptions he gave Congress.

In July 1870, Hayden walked into the Jackson Brothers Photography studio in Omaha, Nebraska. Hayden had seen the studio's owner, William Jackson, once before in Cheyenne, Wyoming. He knew about Jackson's skill with a camera. But it wasn't until Hayden visited the studio that he saw many of Jackson's striking images up close.

Jackson specialized in photographing the mountains, valleys, plateaus, mesas, and rivers of the western United States. This included the Rocky Mountains. The photographs were, Hayden realized, the work of a man who knew and loved the wilderness.

After seeing Jackson's work, Hayden asked him to come along on the journey as a photographer. Hayden also invited Thomas Moran, a painter from Philadelphia, Pennsylvania. The group prepared to set out from Ogden, Utah, in early 1871.

The Colter Stone

In 1931, William Beard lived on a farm near Tetonia, Idaho. This is near the state line with Wyoming. One day, Beard dug up a head-shaped chunk of gray stone. It had the name "John Colter" inscribed on one side and "1808" on the other.[5] John Colter was a real explorer, but he left no records of his travels through the region. If it's real, the "Colter Stone" may be the only evidence of the path Colter took on his way to the Bighorn River through what is now Yellowstone National Park. There's no proof that Colter left the stone. But many historians point out that Beard knew nothing about Colter and was an unlikely hoaxer.

Hayden's Report

The Hayden expedition spent about a month in what is now Yellowstone National Park. Later in 1871, Hayden returned to Washington, DC, with a report on the Yellowstone region. The report described the region's strange geological features and natural beauty. Hayden suggested protecting the land. Instead of using the area for settlement, farming, or mining, Yellowstone would be kept in its natural state, like a park. Anyone from the United States who could manage to get there would have the chance to visit this protected area.

> **The entire surface is perfectly bare of vegetation and hot. . . . I attempted to walk about among these simmering vents, and broke through to my knees, covering myself with hot mud, to my great pain and subsequent inconvenience.**[7]
>
> ***—Ferdinand Hayden, describing Yellowstone's mud springs and geysers in his 1871 report to Congress***

To support his case, Hayden displayed Moran's paintings and Jackson's photographs. Moran had created several oil paintings of Yellowstone Falls and other features in the area. Jackson had taken about 400 photographs.[6] The prints showed lakes, geysers, hot springs, waterfalls, and other wonders set against a sweeping landscape of mountains, canyons, and forested basins.

For many Americans, the western frontier still seemed like a distant and dangerous place for recreation. Most easterners knew about the region only from newspaper stories about cattle thieves, American Indian battles, and the struggles of farmers. Setting aside land for the public's benefit was a new idea at the time. But Congress had already passed an example with the Yosemite Act of 1864, signed into law by President Abraham Lincoln. This law protected Yosemite Falls and the surrounding region from settlement, turning over management of the area to the state of California.

Thomas Moran made watercolor sketches of the Yellowstone landscape during the Hayden expedition. Later, he used those to make large oil paintings, including an 1872 painting titled *Grand Canyon of the Yellowstone*.

The Hayden expedition report, along with the images created by Moran and Jackson, was successful. It persuaded the majority of Congress to support Hayden's idea. Congress passed the Yellowstone National Park Protection Act in early 1872.

The act says, "The headwaters of the Yellowstone River . . . is hereby reserved and withdrawn from settlement, occupancy, or sale . . . and dedicated and set apart as a public park or pleasuring-ground for the benefit and enjoyment of the people."[8] President Ulysses S. Grant signed the act into law on March 1, 1872. With this law, Yellowstone became the country's first national park.

Jim Bridger's Yellowstone

Jim Bridger was a frontiersman from Virginia who knew the western territories well. He was also knowledgeable about the upper Yellowstone River region. He explored this area several times in the 1830s and 1840s. Bridger never made any formal reports to the government. Nor did he write down his experiences. Instead, he told stories in saloons and around campfires. Describing Yellowstone's petrified forests, Bridger spoke of "petrified birds that sang petrified songs."[9] Although Bridger's stories were based on what he knew, he often stretched the truth. This made many people skeptical of stories about the upper Yellowstone region.

Protecting Yellowstone

The 1872 act established Yellowstone as a national park, but the government didn't set aside money to protect or

Early tourists arrived at Yellowstone National Park by train, entering the park at a train station in Gardiner, Montana. They were then shuttled around the park in horse-drawn stagecoaches or wagons.

manage it. There was no federal park service in the 1800s, either. Although the land was legally protected from settlement, no laws protected the natural features that made Yellowstone unique. Nor were there bans on mining or hunting in the park.

Yellowstone was still a very remote place too. No roads led to or through the park. There were trails for pack animals and guides along with ancient tracks used by American Indian peoples hunting in or migrating through the area. The only ways to reach the park were on horseback, by wagon train, or by stagecoach. Early visitors had to hire guides and live in tent camps. There were no hotels, stores, or restaurants at the park.

Eventually, the government began making improvements to the area. The second superintendent of Yellowstone, Philetus Norris, built a few roads and a headquarters at Mammoth Hot Springs. Commercial development also took place, with hot spring baths and a laundry service built near Old Faithful.

However, protecting the park's wilderness was a tall order. People set up camp in the park without permission. Poachers threatened wild bison and antelope herds. To deal with these problems, the government assigned the

In 2021, Yellowstone National Park welcomed about 4.86 million visitors. It was the busiest year in the park's history.

job of protecting the park to the US Army in 1886. In 1891, the military built a guardhouse, barracks, and officers' quarters near the park's northern entrance. Sandstone quarried at the park was used to build Fort Yellowstone.

To further address the problems, the Yellowstone Park Protection Act was passed in 1894. It set fines and jail sentences for anyone found hunting, damaging natural features, or engaging in illegal activities in the park. Over the following years, the US Army built several new outposts in the park. In 1910, 324 soldiers were stationed in Yellowstone.[10] The National Park Service (NPS) took over management of the park in 1918, just two years after the government agency was created.

Over the next century, the number of annual visitors to Yellowstone National Park steadily increased. Better roads were built, allowing tourists to access the park from all directions. Small resort towns popped up near the park entrances, where hotels, restaurants, and outfitters opened.

Since 2008, the number of visitors has reached more than three million every year.[11] In 2024, the park welcomed more than 4.6 million visitors.[12] Despite this heavy traffic, Yellowstone National Park has survived as one of the last stretches of untamed wilderness in the lower 48 states.

CHAPTER TWO

GETTING THERE AND GETTING AROUND

Visitors to Yellowstone National Park have a big task ahead of them. There are mountains, prairies, and forests to explore. There are geothermal features and wildlife to see. Getting to the park and getting around inside the park require some research and planning.

The park lies in a remote stretch of the northern Rocky Mountains, far from the nearest interstate highway. The modern boundaries of the park enclose 3,472 square miles (8,992 sq km) in northwestern Wyoming, southern Montana, and eastern Idaho. Visitors can arrive at the park by road through one of five official entrances.[1]

Most visitors arrive at Yellowstone National Park in private vehicles. The park allows cars, vans, and campers.

When visitors arrive at one of Yellowstone's entrances, they must purchase a physical park pass or present a prepurchased online pass. During busy months, guests may have to wait in long lines at the entrances.

Motorcyclists are also welcome. Guests on bicycles or e-bicycles can share the roads with vehicles. When roads are closed due to weather conditions, the park sometimes still allows bicycles to travel on them.

In the winter, the best—and sometimes only—way to get around is by snowmobile or snowcoach. Snowcoaches are small buses equipped with tracks or special wheels that allow them to drive through deep snow and over ice. The park also offers guided snowmobile trips.

Checking In

Like all national parks, Yellowstone charges an entrance fee. For vehicles, the fee is $35 for a seven-day pass. For motorcycles and snowmobiles, the fee is $30 for one passenger and one driver. Guests who arrive on bicycles, on skis, or on foot must pay a $20 fee. Annual park passes cost $70. These allow the pass holder and up to three other adults to visit the park as many times as they like in one vehicle. Guests who are 62 or older can get an $80 Senior Lifetime Pass or a $20 Senior Annual Pass.[3] Some people can get free passes to national parks. Military members can get free annual and sometimes lifetime passes. So can people with disabilities and families with a fourth grader. Passes can be purchased at visitor centers or online.

The North Entrance is the only one open year-round. This entrance is also the closest to the nearest major airport in Bozeman, Montana. Many visitors fly to Bozeman and then rent a car for the two-hour drive to Yellowstone.[2] The West Entrance is the park's busiest entrance. It is located near Old Faithful and other major attractions. Some visitors fly to Salt Lake City, Utah, and then take a highway journey to the West Entrance. The drive takes about four hours and 45 minutes.[4] To reach Yellowstone's South Entrance, visitors must first pass through Grand Teton National Park.

When arriving at Yellowstone National Park, a visitor center is a good place to start. Visitor centers are located at each park entrance, and five more are scattered around the park at sites such as Old Faithful.[5] The visitor center staff can inform guests about weather conditions, road

At the Old Faithful Visitor Education Center, guests can shop for souvenirs, talk to park rangers, and see exhibits focused on Yellowstone's geothermal features. People can also enjoy views of Old Faithful from the center's windows.

and campground closings, wildlife sightings, and even the timing of upcoming geyser eruptions. Many visitor centers also post a schedule of ranger-guided tours and presentations.

Best Time of Year

When planning a trip to Yellowstone National Park, visitors must consider the season, the climate, and the crowds. Summer is the busiest time in the park. There are often crowds at the visitor centers, busy traffic on the roads, and big groups at the popular geysers and hot springs.

Late spring and early fall are quieter seasons at Yellowstone, and many people believe these are the ideal times to visit. The park gradually opens in late spring. This is a good time to view wildlife. Bison, for example, typically give birth to calves in the spring. The young

Junior Ranger Program

The NPS operates a junior ranger program in Yellowstone and other major national parks. This program is geared toward younger visitors. It includes classes, guided hikes on the park's boardwalks, and a booklet of fun activities. At the end of the program, junior rangers earn a wooden badge. For extra credit, there's even a Junior Ranger Wildlife Olympics held at the park in the summer. Information about the program is available online and at Yellowstone's visitor centers.

Off the Beaten Path

Yellowstone Llama Treks

There's more than one way to hike a trail in Yellowstone National Park. Many visitors enjoy the scenery on foot or on horseback. But in recent years, a new trail animal has been introduced to the park: the South American llama. Park management has licensed local outfitters to offer llama treks and hikes within park boundaries. Several outfitters offer these experiences, including Yellowstone Llamas and Wildland Trekking.

On a llama trek, each hiker leads a single llama. The animals carry packs and portable chairs and tables for picnics in the wilderness. Some llama treks last about half a day. Others are multiday adventures that lead visitors deep into the backcountry wilderness.

Llamas have been imported from South America to the United States since the 1980s. They are easy to train and lead. The gentle animals are tough and durable, making them well adapted to Yellowstone's steep trails and high elevations.

Llamas make ideal working companions that allow hikers to traverse the park while carrying just a small day pack or nothing at all. With their excellent sense of smell, hearing, and vision, llamas also provide a unique safety feature. They can help alert hikers to wildlife in the vicinity.

bison have lush grass to feed on, and their mothers produce more milk during this time. In the fall, the crowds start to thin. By the end of October, hotels in the park are closed for the season. Deciduous trees change color while temperatures grow cooler. At the park's higher elevations, snow begins to fall.

Yellowstone National Park often has tough winter weather, with heavy snowfall and subzero temperatures.

Yellowstone's snowcoaches are heated to keep guests warm as they travel throughout the park. Many snowcoach tours take guests to and from the Old Faithful Snow Lodge and Mammoth Hot Springs Hotel.

The roads inside the park, as well as many mountain roads in the region surrounding the park, close for the season. This means it can be difficult to access the park in winter. However, the park is less crowded during this time. Some people also visit in winter to enjoy sports such as cross-country skiing, snowmobiling, and snowshoeing. Others travel around the park by snowcoach.

> **Being a seasonal park ranger . . . was one of the most challenging experiences, one of the greatest jobs I ever had. . . . Now it seems more like fun than hard work, though we had plenty of both.**[7]
>
> ***—President Gerald R. Ford in a speech delivered at Old Faithful, 1976***

Four entrances and most roads in the park are closed from November through April.[6] The only entrance available during this time can be reached via US Highway 89, the road that passes through the northern and western reaches of the park. This road links the North Entrance with Tower Junction and Cooke City, Montana.

Lodging

For visitors hoping to stay the night, there are lodging options both inside the park and in the "gateway towns" near the park entrances. These towns lie just outside the park on the major roads. Some visitors opt for a full western experience by staying at a nearby guest ranch. For short stays, private homes are also available to rent through online travel platforms.

The Lake Yellowstone Hotel is the oldest hotel in the park. Guests can stay in the main hotel building or in the Sandpiper Lodge, which sits next door. There are cabins on the property too.

Canyon Lodge is another option. It is near Canyon Village, the main stop for those visiting the Grand Canyon of the Yellowstone. Visitors staying in Canyon Village can hike up nearby Mount Washburn to enjoy spectacular views. Or they can look for wildlife in Hayden Valley.

The Grant Village hotel sits on the western shore of Lake Yellowstone, not far from Old Faithful. The most famous hotel in Yellowstone National Park is also located near this site. It is called the Old Faithful Inn. The massive log structure dates back to 1904. It includes 327 rooms that are available for overnight guests.[8] Some of the rooms have a direct view of the famous geyser.

On the northern shore of Yellowstone Lake are Lake Village and Bridge Bay. Stores, ranger stations, and hotels are located here. Bridge Bay is also home to campgrounds and a boat marina. Visitors can find a gas station and

Lake Yellowstone Hotel is known for its large columns and bright yellow color. It offers a variety of suites, guest rooms, and cabins.

an RV park at Fishing Bridge. In the gateway town of West Yellowstone, visitors can find geysers, hot springs, and campgrounds.

Supplies and Restaurants

There are several places where visitors can load up on supplies in and around Yellowstone. General stores are open at the large road junctions in the park, including Canyon Village, Tower Fall, and Old Faithful Village. Here, customers can buy groceries, gas, camping supplies, bear spray, maps, and guides. Some stores sell clothing too.

Visitors can also find stores in the gateway towns. Shops in these towns usually offer supplies or gas at lower prices than places in the park. Jackson at the South

The Old Faithful Inn Dining Room serves breakfast, lunch, and dinner. The restaurant features a large stone fireplace and log beams on the ceiling.

Entrance, Livingston at the North Entrance, and Cody at the East Entrance are all home to Walmart stores and small grocery stores.

Cooking meals while on vacation isn't everyone's favorite activity. Luckily, there are canteens, coffee shops, and full-service restaurants in and around Yellowstone's hotels. Guests can visit the hotels' front desks to learn more about restaurant hours, menus, and reservations. Canyon Village's Canyon Lodge is home to the Falls Café, the M66 Lounge, and the Canyon Lodge Eatery. At Washburn Lodge, park guests can eat at the

Washburn Lookout. Another option is the Lake House at Grant Village. These restaurants close during the winter.

For people visiting Yellowstone in the off-season, there are several dining choices at Madison Junction. These include the Warming Hut and the Map Room at the Mammoth Hotel. The Old Faithful area stays busy throughout the year too. At the Old Faithful Snow Lodge, visitors can eat at the Geyser Grill or the Obsidian Dining Room.

Picnics are another option for park guests. They can enjoy packed lunches at one of Yellowstone's 52 picnic areas.[9] All picnickers must follow park rules. Open fires are not allowed, and only portable cookstoves or charcoal grills can be used. Visitors must keep food in their vehicles when they aren't eating. They must also remember to leave no food scraps behind and to never feed wildlife.

Damage Control

Although Yellowstone is a protected area, the park still faces some threats. By the 2020s, four million people were visiting the park each year.[10] These high numbers of visitors can take a toll on the land, causing erosion and damaging plants. Sometimes visitors damage the park's natural features too. One example is Morning Glory Pool, a site in the Upper Geyser Basin. In the past, this hot pool was a vivid shade of blue. Over the years, visitors have thrown thousands of coins and other objects into the pool. The debris blocked the natural water conduits underground. The pool's deep blue color gradually faded, and it turned green and yellow.

CHAPTER THREE

EXPLORING YELLOWSTONE'S VOLCANIC HISTORY

Many of Yellowstone's visitors are drawn to the park's geology. Yellowstone is home to unique geological features such as geysers, lava flows, and petrified trees. Guests can get maps of these features at the park's visitor centers. Park rangers also conduct guided tours of geological sights, while informational signs throughout the park provide details about how these features formed.

Yellowstone is home to several geothermal basins. These are areas in which groups of geothermal features are active. The park's basins include the Hayden Valley Geyser Basin, Norris Geyser Basin, Lower Geyser Basin, Mammoth Hot Springs, Midway Geyser Basin, Upper Geyser Basin, and West Thumb Geyser Basin.

The Norris Geyser Basin is one of the hottest and oldest geothermal areas in Yellowstone National Park. It is home to many geysers and hot springs.

Trails, turnouts, and parking lots along the Grand Loop Road allow park guests to easily reach these sites.

The many geysers and other geothermal features that visitors see at Yellowstone are powered by an active volcano beneath the land's surface. Scientists expect this volcano to erupt again in the future. While many visitors know about the park's volcanic history, few realize just how big the Yellowstone volcano is.

Petrified Trees

Yellowstone National Park contains deposits of petrified trees, which were formed by volcanic activity. About 50 million years ago, volcanic eruptions took place on the Absaroka Mountains in the eastern half of the park. The heat melted snow on the mountaintops. This sent lahars, or waves of superheated mud, tumbling down the mountains. Mineral-rich water from the lahars seeped into the trees, transforming them into stone over the course of many years. Today, visitors can reach Yellowstone's largest petrified tree deposit by hiking a trail that leads away from the Northeast Entrance Road. Park officials protect some trees by fencing them off, and visitors are prohibited from removing pieces of the trees.

The volcano has erupted several times in the past, with the most recent eruption occurring about 640,000 years ago. It created an immense crater, or caldera, on Earth's surface. The caldera covers about 1,500 square miles (3,900 sq km) in the center of Yellowstone National Park.[1] At Washburn Hot Springs, an overlook allows visitors to see a level ridge of land that forms one of the caldera's rims. The scene reminds guests that the park's entire landscape once erupted in hot lava and immense clouds of superheated gas—and that it will do so again someday.

Geysers

Yellowstone National Park is home to 500 active geysers, which is about half of all known geysers on Earth.[2] There are more geysers in Yellowstone than in any other place on the planet. A geyser is a column of spouting steam and water. The water is heated in underground reservoirs. Yellowstone has plenty of this subsurface water, which comes from rain or heavy spring snowmelts. In geyser basins, a single large water source feeds several different geysers lying close together.

To erupt, geysers need underground hot springs. The water in these springs flows in narrow vertical channels whose bottoms are formed of hot rock. The rock is heated

Lodgepole Pines

Visitors to Yellowstone National Park often notice many tall, skinny pine trees in the area. In some of the park's forests, these trees have taken over completely. They have long, bare trunks and shallow roots. The forest floors beneath them have few grasses, shrubs, or wildflowers. These trees are lodgepole pines, and there's a good reason for their abundance. These trees thrive on soil that is rich in volcanic rock. A big stand of lodgepole pines signals that there is a deposit of volcanic rock belowground.

by the underlying volcano. Steam rises in the form of bubbles, trapping the water in underground chambers as the pressure builds. The geyser begins to overflow around its opening. This causes the pressure to drop, making the water boil. A giant mass of steam forces the water up and out through a vent in Earth's surface. The geyser erupts in a spectacular column of water and steam.

Some geysers at Yellowstone National Park, including Castle Geyser, are marked with signs that list their names and their predicted eruption times.

Don't Miss It!

Upper Geyser Basin

The Upper Geyser Basin is home to Old Faithful, Yellowstone's most famous geyser. This area has the largest concentration of geysers on the planet. It includes paved bike paths and miles of boardwalks and trails that lead to 150 geothermal features, including the deep-blue Heart Spring and the Beehive Geyser, a cone geyser that can spout water 200 feet (61 m) in the air when it erupts.[3]

The Upper Geyser Basin is also home to Grand Geyser and Sawmill Geyser. Sawmill Geyser is part of a big underground system of waterways that feed into many features, including hot springs. Another highlight of the basin is the Riverside Geyser, which erupts across the surface of the Firehole River.

The nearby Old Faithful Visitor Education Center predicts eruption times for five geysers in the Upper Geyser Basin. This makes it easy for visitors to plan a hike that will include at least one eruption. A full loop walk through the Upper Geyser Basin takes at least half a day and covers six miles (9.7 km).[4] The route offers an easy hike. But visitors can also make a short, steep climb up to Observation Point for a sweeping view of the entire basin.

There are two types of geysers in Yellowstone National Park. Cone geysers erupt through a single vent in the surface, usually in the form of a tall column. Fountain geysers erupt in several spots from a pool of hot water.

Some geysers are predictable. They erupt regularly because their underground structures, water pressure, and temperatures are stable. But other geysers are unpredictable. Some may erupt every few years, while others change frequency with the seasons.

Old Faithful is Yellowstone National Park's best-known feature. One of the most famous geysers in the world, it erupts regularly about every 90 minutes.[5] This reliable pattern is what gave the geyser its name. Old Faithful is located on the western side of the park in the Upper Geyser Basin. This is a popular stop on the Grand Loop Road, a route along which visitors can take in dozens of other geothermal features.

> **[The geysers] display an exuberance of strange motion and energy admirably calculated to shake up, and surprise, and frighten the dullest observer out of soul-wasting apathy, and make him begin to grow and live again.[6]**
>
> ***—John Muir, naturalist, describing a visit to Yellowstone in 1885***

From Old Faithful, visitors can walk along a boardwalk that runs across the Firehole River to the northwest.

Beyond the river lie more geysers and hot springs. Many of these features are linked through the same underground system of channels and cracks. What visitors see is one big geyser system erupting at several different places.

White Dome Geyser is located in the Lower Geyser Basin. Its eruptions can reach up to 30 feet (9 m) in the air.

Yellowstone's Great Fountain Geyser is in the middle of a pool of water. Its eruptions last 45 to 60 minutes.

Many of Yellowstone's geysers have unique names, such as Beehive Geyser and Castle Geyser. Others have interesting histories. For example, some people used to do laundry at Chinese Spring in the 1880s. Clothing and soap were placed inside the geyser, and then the clothing was retrieved after it erupted. Another geyser lies along the banks of the Firehole River. It is called Riverside Geyser. It erupts about every six hours, firing a cannon of hot water across the river.[7]

North of Old Faithful is Firehole Lake Drive, a three-mile (4.8 km) one-way road that passes near the Great Fountain Geyser and the White Dome Geyser.[8] The White Dome Geyser is a sinter cone. These form when a deposit of a substance called silica builds up from volcanic eruptions, creating a whitish conical mound around a geyser's mouth.

Visitors can follow the Firehole River along the Grand Loop Road, which continues south of Old Faithful. A five-mile (8 km) trail for hiking or biking leads from the road to the Lone Star Geyser. This is another geyser with a cone built up around its mouth. It erupts about 45 feet (14 m) in the air every three hours.[9]

More Geyser Basins

The Norris Geyser Basin has two loop trails that park guests can use to visit geysers and other geothermal features.[10] The Porcelain Basin is home to Constant Geyser and Steamboat Geyser. The eruptions of Steamboat Geyser can reach 400 feet (122 m) in height, making it the world's tallest geyser.[11]

The West Thumb Geyser Basin is located 27 miles (44 km) from the park's eastern entrance. West Thumb is the name given to a thumb-shaped peninsula that stretches into Lake Yellowstone. Guests can explore two short loop trails in this basin.[12] However, because there are fewer famous features along these trails, they draw fewer visitors than the more popular trails at the Norris and Upper Geyser Basins.

All Aboard

There's more than one way for visitors to see Lake Yellowstone. The park offers guided tours of the lake aboard the *Lake Queen II*, a touring craft that departs several times daily from the Bridge Bay Marina. This is located on Bridge Bay, just off US Highway 20 in the northeastern corner of the lake. During the tour, passengers learn about the Lake Area District and a sunken boat called the *E. C. Waters*. They also learn about local wildlife and Yellowstone's volcanic history.

In the northeastern stretch of Yellowstone National Park is the Hayden Valley Geyser Basin, which features the popular Mud Volcano Trail. This trail begins at a turnout along the Grand Loop Road. It then passes the Mud Volcano geothermal area, which includes level boardwalks and footpaths that provide easy access and viewing spots for visitors. Several miles northwest of Mud Volcano is Crater Hills, which is accessible only through more rugged and steep trails. This area features small hot springs.

The Mud Volcano Trail leads visitors in a 0.6-mile (1 km) loop around the Mud Volcano area. Guests walk past unique features such as mud pools.

However, in 2016, the park closed Crater Hills to the public after eruptions occurred in the area. According to park rules, backcountry geothermal areas are off-limits to visitors unless official trails lead to them.

Geyser Dangers

While viewing Yellowstone's geothermal wonders, it's important for visitors to remember that these features can be very dangerous. Superheated water at springs and geysers can injure or even kill people. Guests are not allowed to bring pets while visiting these features and must supervise young children at all times.

Warning signs posted throughout Yellowstone's geothermal areas remind visitors to stay on marked trails at all times. They also warn guests to never touch geothermal features or throw things into them.

Boardwalks provide a safe way for visitors to walk near and around the park's most popular geysers and springs. If a person strays away from the boardwalks and gets too close to the geysers, a thin layer of rock can give way under their weight. Scalding water may lie beneath.

Scientists and park rangers keep a close watch on the geothermal features of Yellowstone National Park. They watch for any new or dangerous activity. From time to time, sections of the park are closed because they are not safe for people to visit.

In the summer of 2024, a geothermal explosion occurred at Biscuit Basin, north of Old Faithful. The eruption threw hot rocks, superheated water, steam, and sand hundreds of yards in the air, posing a serious danger to anyone in the vicinity. After the explosion, the littered roads and broken boardwalks in Biscuit Basin were immediately closed for the rest of the 2024 season.

Safety is key at Yellowstone National Park. The park has recorded more than 20 deaths of people who jumped or fell into hot springs.[13] During the long, harsh winters, some park visitors have died from exposure in bad weather conditions. Before exploring an area of Yellowstone, guests should always check for any current travel advisories or weather warnings. Signs at geyser viewing areas and hot spring basins also remind visitors to stay on the boardwalks and trails.

CHAPTER FOUR

YELLOWSTONE'S GEOTHERMAL FEATURES

Geysers are not the only sights to see at Yellowstone. Other geothermal wonders also attract visitors. By using the park's roads and trails, guests can see features such as hot springs, mud pots, and fumaroles. Lava flows, which were created by molten rock moving over the landscape during volcanic eruptions, are also visible.

From a mountaintop or high overlook, visitors can see swirling columns of white steam rising from the plains below. The Crow people once called this area the "land of the burning ground."[1] The steam columns are fumaroles, which are present in the Norris Geyser Basin, on and around Roaring Mountain, and near Mud Volcano.

There are about 2,000 fumaroles in Yellowstone National Park.[2] They contain

Roaring Mountain, which stands at an elevation of 8,152 feet (2,485 m), gets its name from the sounds that its many fumaroles make.

hot, highly acidic water drawn from underground sources. Instead of erupting from time to time like geysers, fumaroles are constantly active, emitting towers of hot water and steam from fissures in the ground.

Fumaroles make hissing and growling noises. Many release noxious and smelly gases, including hydrogen chloride, sulfur dioxide, and hydrogen sulfide. Visitors who want a closer look at active fumaroles can use boardwalks and trails that allow safe passage near the features.

Roaring Mountain lies close to US Highway 89, south of Mammoth Hot Springs and just east of Mount Holmes. A steep slab of grayish, treeless rock rises from the plain. Fumaroles cover some parts of the mountainside, with boiling gases and water hissing and steaming from the vents. The mountain lies above a network of underground channels that lead north from the caldera and eventually beyond Yellowstone National Park's boundaries.

A New Geyser

In a forest along Yellowstone National Park's Observation Point Trail, hikers walk past a single lonely geyser. It is called the Solitary Geyser. At one time, it was no more than an ordinary hot spring. In 1914, water from the spring was used to supply hot water to a hotel swimming pool. But the builders' digging changed the underground waterways, transforming the hot spring into a geyser. Eventually, the hotel swimming pool closed. Today, park officials ban any kind of construction near geothermal features. But the human-made Solitary Geyser still erupts from time to time, shooting a few feet into the air.

Mud Pots

North of Yellowstone Lake along the Grand Loop Road, visitors can follow a turnout to see Mud Volcano. This area holds the park's largest collection of mud pots. Acidic water, steam, and heat lying underneath and around a mud pot melt the surrounding rock, creating a warm pool of clay. A thick slurry forms large bubbles that rise from the ground and then burst several feet in the air. These bubbling mud pools allow hydrogen sulfide gas to escape

The Mud Volcano area's namesake feature is a large crater of bubbling mud. It was once shaped like a cone or dome.

from the hot chambers below, making Mud Volcano smell like rotten eggs.

Park visitors can follow a hiking trail in the Mud Volcano area to see mud pots, hot springs, and other geothermal features. These include the Churning Caldron, Mud Geyser, Mud Caldron, the Sulphur Caldron, and the Grizzly Fumarole. While viewing these features, visitors must be cautious. The mud and water can get hot enough to burn nearby plants and trees. In 1999, one mud pot burst through the asphalt surface of a parking lot, creating what is now known as the Parking Lot Pool.

Near the Mud Volcano area is Dragon's Mouth Spring. This pool of hot water emerges from a fissure in the side of a small cliff. As steam rises from the water, the vent hisses and snorts. The pool got its name because people thought it sounded like a dragon grunting underground.

Eruption Evidence

At other spots in the park, visitors can spot evidence of volcanic eruptions. The caldera created by Yellowstone's last eruption is easier to spot on maps than in person. It covers an oblong plateau of about 30 miles by 45 miles (48 km by 72 km) in the center of the park.[3] The area atop the caldera has no mountain ranges or peaks.

The Shoshone Geyser Basin

The Shoshone Geyser Basin is Yellowstone's largest backcountry geyser site. Hikers can reach it by following the Shoshone Lake Trail, which is 8.5 miles (13.7 km) long. Seasoned hikers can also follow two steep trails to the peak of Mount Washburn, which lies 10,243 feet (3,122 m) above sea level. From the peak, hikers can see up to 50 miles (80 km) over the Grand Canyon of the Yellowstone.[5] On clear days, it's also possible to make out the outlines of the Yellowstone caldera.

In the years following the eruption, superheated rock and volcanic ash filled in the original crater. Since then, lava flows and resurgent domes have also emerged. Visitors can spot the outlines of the caldera from high points in the park, such as the peak of Mount Washburn. This is located between Tower Fall and Canyon Village.

Northeast of Mud Volcano and beyond the northern shores of Lake Yellowstone is the Sour Creek resurgent dome. It looks like a large, rounded hill. Yellowstone's underground magma chamber lies near the surface here. It presses upward, deforming the land. This creates fractures in the ground and frequent small earthquakes.

Another resurgent dome can be found at Yellowstone's Mallard Lake, not far from Old Faithful. The land in and around a resurgent dome can rise and fall by several inches in a single year. Since the mid-1900s, Yellowstone's domes have risen about 3.3 feet (1 m).[4]

From the peak of Mount Washburn, visitors can enjoy a panoramic view of the Yellowstone caldera and parts of its rim. While hiking up the mountain, guests can also see volcanic rock deposits.

The domes serve as an indicator of activity in the park's underground magma chambers. Scientists carefully monitor the domes using instruments that measure changes in height and size. If the domes were to expand upward rapidly, it would mean a large amount of magma is pressing toward the surface. This would be a sign that Yellowstone's next volcano eruption is imminent.

Rhyolite Lava Flows

In addition to the Yellowstone volcano's three major eruptions, there have also been many smaller eruptions in the form of slow-moving lava flows. Scientists identify lava flows as either basaltic or rhyolite. Basaltic flows occur during volcanic explosions, while rhyolite flows move more slowly as magma seeps upward from Earth's interior.

The last magma eruptions in Yellowstone took place between 160,000 and 70,000 years ago. As these large rhyolite flows reached the surface, the molten rock burned and scarred the land. Today, park visitors can see the flows, which look like tall, broad plateaus or dome-like structures. Some consist of bare rock, while others support brush and lodgepole pines. In all, 86 cubic miles (359 cubic km) of rhyolite lava flows have erupted from the Yellowstone volcano.[6]

Scientists identify the park's lava flows with names. The West Yellowstone flow erupted about 110,000 years ago with 10 cubic miles (41 cubic km) of molten rock.[7] Visitors can see this flow along US Highway 20, between the West Entrance and the town of Madison. The Nez Perce Creek flow dates back about 160,000 years.

The Pitchstone Plateau is the most recent of the park's lava flows. It formed about 70,000 years ago. It is in the southwestern corner of the park, in the remote Bechler River backcountry region. Here, visitors can see the swirls and waves created by the molten rock before it cooled and hardened.

Hot Springs

One of Yellowstone's most popular sites is Mammoth Hot Springs. This natural wonder lies near the park's North Entrance and Fort Yellowstone. Since it's located near one of the park's busiest roads, Mammoth Hot Springs draws many visitors throughout the year.

This site features water-filled rock terraces shaped by hot underground springs. Limestone was deposited at the site over millions of years when the region was covered by a sea. When limestone combines with hot water, carbon dioxide in the rock forms carbonic acid. As the heated

Grand Prismatic Spring is more than 121 feet (37 m) deep and between 200 and 330 feet (61 and 100 m) in diameter.

water flows upward, this solution causes the formation of travertine, a sedimentary rock in the ledges and terraces visible from the area's boardwalks.

Many terraces at Mammoth Hot Springs have descriptive names, such as Palette Spring, Cleopatra Terrace, and Jupiter Terrace. Colors appear in the waters surrounding the travertine. The hottest waters appear yellow and white, while cooler waters are green, brown, and orange. These colors are created by microorganisms called thermophiles, which can handle hot environments.

Another colorful sight is Grand Prismatic Spring, which is in the Midway Geyser Basin. It is the largest hot spring in Yellowstone National Park. It is famous for its brightly colored bands of water, which appear in shades of orange, yellow, green, and blue.

A Rainbow of Microbes

Grand Prismatic Spring is considered one of Yellowstone's weirdest sites. Its ring of bright colors makes the spring look like a vivid landscape from an alien planet. The colors in the water come from thermophiles. These microbes live in extreme environments, such as the acidic water that bubbles up from underground volcanic sources. Scientists have identified several thermophiles at Yellowstone, including the orange *metallosphaera* and the yellowish bacteria *hydrogenobaculum*, which consumes hydrogen sulfide and gives off the smell of rotten eggs. Scientists are using these strange life-forms to look for similar organisms on other planets and moons in the solar system.

CHAPTER
FIVE

YELLOWSTONE'S FIRST PEOPLES

In addition to its geological history, Yellowstone National Park also has a rich American Indian history. American Indian peoples have been present in Yellowstone for about 14,000 years. They have lived in the area since the last Ice Age. During this time, an ice sheet covered much of North America, including the region that is now Yellowstone National Park. The period ended about 10,000 years ago.

Archaeologists have uncovered almost 2,000 ancient sites within Yellowstone National Park.[1] The most ancient objects found in the park are stone tools called Clovis points, which date back about 11,000 years. Archaeologists named the Clovis culture after Clovis, New Mexico, where artifacts from these people were

Many American Indian groups traditionally hunted bison in the Yellowstone region. Today, some American Indian tribes have the right to hunt bison that leave the park and cross into Montana.

first discovered. In Yellowstone, archaeologists and visitors have found stone tools and points used for spears and other weapons. Visitors can see samples of these items at museums throughout the park.

Large mammals that roamed the plains and mountain valleys of the Yellowstone area provided American Indians with food, clothing, and shelter for thousands of years. Mountain lions, saber-toothed cats, and woolly mammoths once roamed among the park's geysers and steam vents. Today, mountain lions have moved into the remote mountains, while saber-toothed cats and mammoths have gone extinct.

Several Crow chiefs participated in negotiations for the Fort Laramie Treaty of 1851 and the Fort Laramie Treaty of 1868. The second treaty helped protect their hunting rights.

American Indian peoples of the northern Rocky Mountains included the Shoshone, Crow, Lakota, Blackfoot, Bannock, and Nimiipuu. These nations hunted and gathered edible plants in what is now Yellowstone National Park and its surrounding territories. The Tukudika band of Shoshone lived in the area's higher elevations. For many early American Indian peoples, the upper Yellowstone region was an important source of obsidian, which was used to make tools and weapons. These peoples now live on reservations in Montana, Idaho, and South Dakota.

In 1851, the US government made a land agreement with American Indian peoples in the Yellowstone area. The Fort Laramie Treaty of 1851 granted land east of the Yellowstone River to the Crow. In this treaty, the US government also recognized the right of the Crow and other tribes to hunt on any unoccupied land.

But as more miners and settlers moved through the area, conflict between white settlers and American Indians threatened to disrupt the peace. In the 1880s, the US government forced the Tukudika to move out of the area. Tukudika now live on a Shoshone reservation in Idaho.

During Yellowstone National Park's early years, its superintendents sought to keep American Indians away from tourists. They discouraged American Indians from using the park's lands for hunting or gathering. They also spread false tales that American Indians were fearful of the area's geysers and hot springs. When the US Army took control of the park in 1886, the presence of soldiers was meant to keep American Indians out of the park.

Returning to the Land

For the Shoshone and Bannock, the Yellowstone area was an important place for hunting. It was also a link between their ancestral lands to the west and north and the bison range of the Great Plains. The tribes' rights to hunt and fish on "unoccupied lands" were recognized by the Fort Bridger Treaty of 1868.[3] However, the US government claims that land designated as a national park is occupied. Today, many American Indians want to reclaim some of their rights. The ongoing re-indigenization movement aims to allow American Indians to return to their original lands in some capacity. They may be allowed to hunt on the land or gather plants for ceremonial purposes.

American Indian Sites and Trails

Park guests who are curious about Yellowstone's American Indian history can see a variety of artifacts and archaeological sites in the park. Archaeologists have discovered hundreds of ancient campsites along the shores of Yellowstone Lake. In one study along the lakeshore, a research team found a scraper, a knife, and several arrowheads within an hour of beginning their search.[2] Scraping tools found near Nymph

Lake were analyzed and found to have traces of deer, bear, and rabbit blood.

Visitors can also explore American Indian history on hiking trails in the park. Today, hikers traveling along the course of the Yellowstone River and other rivers follow very old trails. These tracks were once ancient highways. They were present when the first expedition groups arrived in the area in the 1800s. The trails may have been in use for thousands of years before that time.

One part of the Nez Perce National Historic Trail is called Lolo Pass. At the Lolo Pass Visitor Center, located on the Idaho–Montana border, visitors can see a bronze statue honoring the Nez Perce Tribe's 1877 journey.

> **"Pretty much anywhere you'd want to pitch a tent, there are artifacts. Like us, Native Americans liked to camp on flat ground, close to water, with a beautiful view.[4]**
>
> ***—Doug MacDonald, archaeologist, on Yellowstone"***

Another important trail that crosses through Yellowstone National Park is the Nez Perce National Historic Trail. The Nimiipuu, called Nez Perce by European traders, used this trail while fleeing from the US Army in 1877. They fled to avoid being forcibly moved to reservations. The group traveled across the northern half of what is now Yellowstone National Park and over the Absaroka Mountains to Montana. To commemorate this event, Nimiipuu hold ceremonies in the park each year. Visitors can also hike or drive along parts of the trail.

American Indian Structures

Guests can see several American Indian structures in Yellowstone National Park too. These include wickiups, which are temporary shelters made of branch frames and bark or animal hides. Crow, Shoshone, and other peoples built wickiups when they visited the Yellowstone area to hunt or fish. The shelters may also have been used to protect families or animals during winter storms.

Although wickiups are fragile, a few have reportedly survived in the park. These shelters aren't marked on park maps, so visitors must find them on their own or ask an employee at one of the visitor centers for directions. There are said to be several wickiups along Wickiup Creek in the northwestern corner of the park. Others can be seen at Mammoth Hot Springs and in the Gallatin Mountains. Little is known about the origin or authenticity of the wickiups seen in the park.

From time to time, a visitor or park ranger hiking in Yellowstone's backcountry stumbles across an unknown wickiup or even a camp. The Pitchstone Plateau is said to be home to several wickiups. This area in the southwestern region of the park can be reached by trails along the Fall and Bechler Rivers. Wickiups are most likely to be found near the park's original American Indian trails.

Ancient History

Many archaeological discoveries have been made at the Fishing Bridge area along the shores of Yellowstone Lake. Discoveries include hearths, burial sites, tools, and weapons. Studies by University of Montana archaeologists have turned up thousands of artifacts. Ancient burial sites have also been found. In 1996, a fisherman in Yellowstone National Park found a human skeleton along a lakeshore. He contacted park officials, who tested the bones. The body turned out to be nearly 1,000 years old. Based on how the body was oriented, American Indian elders believed it to be a Crow person. A reburial ceremony was held at the spot where the body was found.

Visitors can learn about wickiups and other American Indian structures at Yellowstone National Park's Albright Visitor Center.

Stone circles also have been found along rivers and in higher elevations within the park. American Indian peoples may have used these circles as ceremonial sites or as corrals for horses and other animals. Some stone circles served as foundations for structures.

One example is the Airport Rings site near Gardiner, Montana, just north of the Montana–Wyoming state line. Archaeologists believe that heavy stones found in a circle at the site marked the base of a shelter known as a tepee. The stones held down the bottom edges of the bison hides that covered the tepee's cone of long, straight poles.

Yellowstone National Park visitors can also see the Old Faithful Petroglyphs. This site, located in the Upper Geyser

Basin, was first discovered and photographed by a tourist in 1977. Visitors who are curious to see the rock art can ask for directions at the Old Faithful Visitor Education Center.

Although petroglyphs are common in the surrounding region, the Old Faithful Petroglyphs are the only known rock art within Yellowstone. The glyphs feature circular designs that resemble stylized wheels. There is an ongoing debate among historians over whether the art is of American Indian origin.

Many visitors come to Yellowstone National Park in search of American Indian artifacts, sites, and remains. These are most common in mountain foothills, along streams or lakes, and at the mouths of canyons. Park officials don't discourage visitors from looking for these sites. But people should remember to be respectful, since many of the sites hold spiritual or historical significance for American Indians in the region. Park officials strictly ban moving or removing any object, either natural or human-made, found inside the park.

Museums and Visitor Centers

Many artifacts related to American Indian history are displayed at museums within Yellowstone National Park. One is the Albright Visitor Center. Originally used as housing for military officers, this building was constructed in 1909 near the park's northeastern entrance. It is the only visitor center in the park that is open year-round. It houses exhibits focused on wildlife and American Indian history. Guests can also see artifacts at the Old Faithful Visitor Education Center and at the Norris Geyser Basin Museum, which is located at the Norris Geyser Basin entrance.

In 2024, demonstrations at the Yellowstone Tribal Heritage Center included knapping flint, making drums, weaving, and quilting.

Visitors can further explore American Indian history at the Yellowstone Tribal Heritage Center, which is near the Old Faithful Visitor Education Center. Here, American Indian presenters and artists give demonstrations on traditional arts and crafts, including beadwork, quillwork, jewelry making, photography, watercolor painting, and moccasin making. Visitors can learn sign language or listen to presenters share legends.

The center also offers traditional music, dance performances, and demonstrations of American Indian games and sports. Guests can sign up for a guided plant walk too. A Heritage Center guide leads guests around the Old Faithful area, where they learn about plants used for medicines and food. In 2024, 27 people presented at the Heritage Center.[5]

A Rare Birth

In early June 2024, a white bison calf was born in Yellowstone National Park's Lamar Valley. Bison calves are usually born at this time of year, but it is very rare for the animals to be white in color. It was the first time in the park's history that such a calf had been seen. For the Lakota people, the birth of a white bison calf is an important religious event. It foretells better times ahead if the people take good care of the land and its animals. The Lakota people held a ceremony near the park to celebrate the occasion. Attendees celebrated the calf with dances, drum circles, and storytelling. Tribal leaders also revealed the calf's name, Wakan Gli, which means "return sacred."

CHAPTER SIX

WILDLIFE IN YELLOWSTONE

Yellowstone National Park is home to the largest, most diverse community of free-ranging mammals in North America. There are 67 species of mammals and nearly 300 species of birds.[1] Many visitors come to Yellowstone just to catch a glimpse of the region's wildlife.

Large herds of bison, elk, moose, and bighorn sheep roam Yellowstone National Park. Black bears and brown bears can sometimes be spotted hunting and fishing alone or in small family groups. Bobcats and lynx live and hunt in the park's mountainous regions. Mountain lions also live in the area's high elevations, avoiding human contact. From a safe distance, park visitors may even spot packs of hungry wolves looking for prey.

In Yellowstone National Park, it's common to encounter bison crossing or walking along the roads. Drivers should give the animals plenty of room and drive slowly.

Don't Miss It!

Lamar Valley

Yellowstone National Park is considered one of the best places to view wildlife in North America. Within the park, the top location for wildlife watching is Lamar Valley. This is in the northeastern corner of the park. The Lamar River, which is a tributary of the Yellowstone River, runs 40 miles (64 km) through the valley.[2]

The landscape consists of gentle hills and sagebrush prairies. Grazing bison wander the valley in large herds, accompanied by antelope and elk. Patient viewers may also spot bears, wolves, moose, and coyotes roaming in the valley. Mount Washburn looms to the south, while the majestic Absaroka Mountains rise on the eastern horizon.

Access to and through Lamar Valley is easy. There are turnouts for cars and several picnic spots. Many short hiking trails lead away from US Highway 212. This runs between Tower Junction in the west and Cooke City, Montana, just beyond the park's northern limit.

Park officials provide tips for getting the best views of wildlife in Lamar Valley. Many recommend using a spotting scope. Guests can also bring high-powered binoculars.

There are several popular wildlife-watching locations within Yellowstone National Park. One is Lamar Valley in the northeast. It is the lowest and warmest part of the park, and a variety of animals congregate there. Lamar Valley is also the only area in the park that has a road open all year.

Other good wildlife-watching spots include the Hayden Valley and Mammoth Hot Springs, where bison, elk, and moose graze during the winter. Several hiking trails in the park are also known for being wildlife hot spots. These include the Old Faithful Observation Point Loop and trails around Fairy Falls and Mystic Falls.

Wildlife activity in Yellowstone National Park varies with the seasons. Spring is the calving season, when bison give birth. The elk mating season, or the rut, takes place in September and October. Elk gather around Mammoth

Tracking Wildlife

To understand the ranges and population sizes of animals living in Yellowstone National Park, park officials track animals with remote cameras and GPS collars. But people don't need to be park rangers or even visitors to keep tabs on the park's wildlife. They can use apps on their devices to access information about recent wildlife sightings at the park. One app is called Yellowstone Explorer. It displays paw print icons on a detailed map to show sightings in the last day, week, and month. The Parkwolf app provides maps and audio tours that park visitors can use during their visit. It also provides updates on the latest wildlife sightings.

Hot Springs, at the North Entrance, and along the Madison River. Male elk battle each other and let out high-pitched mating calls known as bugles.

There are no cages or fences separating human visitors from wild animals at Yellowstone National Park. Park officials track animals but do not control them. This means that finding and viewing animals often requires patience. Visitors who hope to spot bison, elk, or bears should arrive at the park early in the day. These animals are most active at dawn. Equipment such as binoculars or spotting scopes can also help visitors get a good view.

Bison

Bison once roamed the western United States and the Great Plains region in vast herds. The animals were hunted nearly to extinction by the late 1800s. After the US Army took control of Yellowstone, soldiers captured poacher Edgar Howell and posed for a picture with some of Howell's bison heads. The photo caused a public outcry. It led to the Yellowstone Park Protection Act of 1894, which banned all hunting in Yellowstone.

In the mid-1900s, the park's small bison herd gradually grew. Park managers moved bison from private herds into Yellowstone. In early 2024, there were about 4,550 wild

Sometimes bison can be spotted near Yellowstone's boardwalks and geothermal areas. In colder months, the animals may gather near geysers and hot springs to stay warm.

bison roaming the park.[3] This is the largest population of wild bison in the United States.

Adult male bison can reach about 2,000 pounds (907 kg), while females are about half that weight.[4] The animals' short, curved horns help them defend themselves against wolves and grizzly bears, their main predators. Bison graze throughout the day on grass, sedges, and other plants in Yellowstone's meadows and plains.

Bison move in large herds during the warm months but break up into smaller groups in winter. They grow thick coats of fur that keep their bodies well insulated in cold weather. The large hump on the back of a bison's neck has muscles that make it easier for the bison to plow its head through deep snow in search of winter grass. In winter, bison also congregate around springs, which provide warmth and access to open, grassy areas.

> **Skilled wildlife watchers . . . don't rely on chance alone. They know that animals favor certain areas. . . . Elk go where the grazing is good, and wolves follow the elk. . . . Bison take the easiest route from place to place.[5]**
>
> ***—From National Geographic's*** **Secrets of the National Parks**

Visitors to Yellowstone National Park can easily spot bison at any time of the year. During the calving season in April and May, visitors can take wildlife tours that bring them to prime viewing spots to see baby bison. Guests who witness a bison birth watch the newborn as it struggles to its feet and begins walking. There may be a threatening, hungry wolf pack nearby. The adult bison gather close together and rush, heads down and horns out, to fend off any attackers.

The bison's range in Yellowstone National Park varies with the seasons. During the summer, the animals are commonly found in Lamar Valley, Hayden Valley, Firehole River Valley, and along the Yellowstone River.

Between September and May, the bison migrate to the park's lower elevations. Prime winter viewing spots include Pelican Valley, which is north of Yellowstone Lake, and a large range surrounding Mammoth Hot Springs at the park's northern end.

Watching for Wolves

Gray wolves have thrived in Yellowstone since the 1990s, when several wildlife and park agencies reintroduced them to the area. In 2024, officials counted at least 124 wolves living in ten different packs throughout the park.[6] Wolf trackers have given these packs names. These include Junction Butte, Wapiti Lake, Willow Creek, and 8 Mile.

Wolves move about Yellowstone National Park in constant search of prey. They follow wild game, which

Moving Wolves into Yellowstone

By the 1990s, gray wolves had almost disappeared from the lower 48 states. They had been completely hunted out of the Rocky Mountains. Just a few packs survived in northern Michigan and Minnesota. Many farmers and ranchers considered the animals a dangerous nuisance. But in 1995, Yellowstone National Park welcomed 14 wolves that had been captured in Canada's Jasper National Park.[7] The wolves were released in Lamar Valley and left to fend for themselves in their new environment. The wolves spread out in search of prey and bred freely. They became a natural means of balancing the park's deer and elk populations.

Park officials monitor the number of males, females, and pups in each Yellowstone wolf pack. The park's Wapiti Lake pack formed in 2014.

means visitors are likely to spot them in places where bison, elk, bears, moose, bighorn sheep, and other large mammals graze. One excellent area for wolf watching is Lamar Valley. This area's relatively flat landscape allows visitors to see wolves from far away.

Several private operators offer wolf-watching tours in Yellowstone National Park. Guides pay close attention to wolf reports from park ranger stations and communicate with each other via radio. Using the information they have about wolf sightings, the guides take visitors on a bus tour. The tour group stops along the road to listen for wolf howls.

Winter is the best season for wolf watching at Yellowstone National Park. During this season, wolves are active during the day while hunting for elk. Serious wildlife watchers at the park use high-powered scopes or look for groups of people gathered on the side of the road. A small crowd assembled at a trailhead or turnout usually means something interesting has been spotted.

For more information about Yellowstone's wolves, guests can check out the park's visitor centers. There, they can talk to guides and park rangers, who often know where wolves have been spotted. These employees can direct visitors to good wildlife-watching areas.

Bears

Both black bears and grizzly bears are found throughout Yellowstone National Park. It's common to see bears near the busy boardwalks that lead visitors around geysers and hot springs. Black bears wandering near popular sights go about their business and don't usually pose a threat to visitors.

However, it's not always easy to tell the difference between black bears and grizzly bears, which can both be black or brown in color. Grizzly bears have big shoulder humps, long claws, and back rumps that are lower than their shoulders. Black bears have rumps that are higher than their shoulders. They also have shorter claws meant for climbing.

Yellowstone's grizzly population varies from year to year but can reach as many as 1,000 animals.[8] These bears are most commonly seen in Hayden Valley, in Lamar Valley, and on Mount Washburn. They also favor the park's eastern side, from the eastern entrance to the Fishing Bridge area on Yellowstone Lake. The region of Tower Junction is known as the "Bearmuda Triangle." It's a rare place where black and brown bears coexist.

Visitors hoping to spot a bear have the best luck at dawn or dusk, when bears are most active. During midday, the animals are usually sleeping or inactive. If bears find a large animal carcass, they will gather around it throughout the day. To stay informed about bear activity in Yellowstone, wildlife watchers can talk to

Wildlife in the Air

Yellowstone National Park is home to a variety of birds. Since the earliest records in 1872, about 300 bird species have been spotted in the park. These include waterfowl, raptors, and shorebirds. In 2024, about 150 bird species were known to nest in Yellowstone.[9] Park visitors hoping to spot birds at Yellowstone should know where to look. Eagles and falcons prefer high vantage points such as treetops. Shorebirds stick to beaches and shorelines. Park visitors in search of birds often bring binoculars, notebooks, field guides, and checklists with them. Some use bird-watching apps, such as eBird and iNaturalist.

Grizzly bears usually have one to three cubs. If park visitors spot a female bear with her cubs, they should keep their distance and never come between the mother and her babies.

park rangers at a visitor center. Guests can also strike up conversations at turnouts, where people are often actively looking for wildlife.

Staying Safe

It's important for visitors to remember that Yellowstone is a wilderness, not a zoo. The park's large, free-ranging mammals can be dangerous. While viewing bison, visitors should never try to approach one of the animals. Some park guests have tried to touch bison or pose next to them to take photos. However, the NPS warns that this can be dangerous. Yellowstone's bison are used to cars and crowds but can still be unpredictable. When agitated, bison can become aggressive and charge. They can easily outrun humans.

Many visitors at Yellowstone National Park bring cameras, telescopes, or binoculars to get a close-up view of wildlife. The NPS provides recommendations for photography equipment and wildlife-watching locations on its website.

Bears can also pose a danger to park guests. Bears can't see very well but have an excellent sense of smell, and they'll charge if they feel startled or threatened. Park rangers advise people to never hike alone on the park's trails. This is because most bear attacks happen to solitary hikers. To prevent an unwanted animal encounter, visitors should stay on marked trails and make noise to keep animals away.

The park has very strict rules about viewing and approaching wildlife. Visitors must stay at least 25 yards (23 m) away from bison and elk and 100 yards (91 m) away from bears and wolves.[10] The park also has special instructions for bear encounters. Guests should never run or make sudden movements when within sight of a bear. This can provoke unwelcome encounters.

Leaving food where bears can easily access it or directly feeding bears is also strictly banned in Yellowstone National Park. Feeding a bear or elk may persuade the animal to actively seek out more food at campsites and nearby visitor centers. This increases the possibility of unwanted or dangerous animal encounters. People caught feeding wildlife in the park can be fined and may even face jail time.

CHAPTER SEVEN

HISTORIC LANDMARKS

When Yellowstone National Park was established, the US government started a new policy. It agreed to protect some areas of wilderness. These areas would remain wild so that everyone had a chance to visit them. The law restricted private ownership of land within national parks along with settlement, mining, and farming. In the following years, 62 more national parks were established.[1]

While national parks are designed to protect areas of natural beauty and wilderness, National Historic Landmarks are places that are important to US history. A National Historic Landmark can be a building, the site of an important event, or a battlefield. In order for a site to become a National Historic Landmark, Congress

To view Obsidian Cliff, visitors at Yellowstone National Park can drive by the site on the Grand Loop Road. They can also stop at a roadside pullout that includes a viewpoint and an informational kiosk.

must declare it one. By 2024, there were more than 2,600 National Historic Landmarks. Eight of these are located within Yellowstone National Park.[2]

Obsidian Cliff

One National Historic Landmark in Yellowstone is Obsidian Cliff. This natural landmark was important to American Indian peoples who lived in the region. It was created by a volcanic explosion about 180,000 years ago. Lava from the explosion formed tall vertical columns. The molten rock gradually cooled and hardened into glassy obsidian. American Indians broke rock fragments from the cliff and shaped them into tools.

Yellowstone's Oldest Landmark

The oldest building in Yellowstone National Park is not a hotel or museum. It's the ruins of a log shack lying about 500 yards (457 m) from a backcountry trail in the Lower Geyser Basin.[3] Built as a bathhouse for a nearby swimming hole, the shack dates to 1881. It is called the Queen's Laundry Bathhouse. It was the first building raised for public use in any national park. The log walls of the bathhouse are slowly turning to silica stone from the mineral-rich water that sprays on them from nearby hot springs.

Obsidian from the site has been quarried for about 12,000 years. Today, thousands of small obsidian shards litter the ground at the cliff's base. Obsidian fragments can also be found at old campsites along the park's original foot trails and waterways. Tools and points from Obsidian

Cliff have been found throughout the western United States and Canada. Some have been discovered as far east as the Ohio River valley.

Obsidian Cliff lies about 13 miles (21 km) from Mammoth Hot Springs, east of US Highway 89 in the northeastern section of the park.[4] The cliff has long been an attraction for souvenir hunters. To prevent people from taking artifacts from the site, the NPS closed direct public access to the face of Obsidian Cliff. Today, visitors interested in learning about the site can visit a roadside kiosk along US Highway 89.

Roosevelt Arch and Fort Yellowstone

Another historic landmark in Yellowstone is the Roosevelt Arch, which was built in Gardiner, Montana, in 1903. Yellowstone's directors decided the park needed a big monument to mark the North Entrance. They constructed a large stone arch and named it after Theodore Roosevelt, who was president at the time. A former cattle rancher and hunter, Roosevelt strongly believed in protecting wilderness areas. He visited Yellowstone National Park to give a speech at a ceremony for the arch.

Just west of North Entrance Road is Fort Yellowstone, another National Historic Landmark. It is a large complex

Roosevelt Arch, which stands 50 feet (15 m) tall, includes a plaque inscribed with the phrase "For the Benefit and Enjoyment of the People." These words are from the Yellowstone National Park Protection Act of 1872.

of old military structures. The US Army began building the complex in the 1890s.

In all, 35 buildings at the fort have survived.[5] They date back to the 1890s and early 1900s. Their purpose was to shelter army personnel who were protecting the park. From the fort, army personnel patrolled the roads and trails that led visitors into the park. They were authorized to stop hunters, close businesses such as camps and laundries, and remind souvenir hunters not to collect petrified wood or mineral formations.

Since the creation of the NPS in 1916, the buildings of Fort Yellowstone have remained open to visitors. Guests can see large cavalry barracks, stables, storehouses, a hospital, a guardhouse, officers' quarters, a chapel, and a blacksmith's shop. Visiting the fort brings guests back in time, offering a look at what military life was like more than a century ago.

Old Faithful Inn and Lake Yellowstone Hotel

Two of Yellowstone National Park's hotels are on the list of National Historic Landmarks. One is the Old Faithful Inn, the largest log structure in the country. The hotel, which is located near Old Faithful, stands seven stories tall.[6] Architect Robert Reamer designed the building, which opened to the public in 1904.

> **The only way that the people as a whole can secure to themselves and their children the enjoyment in perpetuity of what the Yellowstone Park has to give is by . . . preserving the scenery, the forests, and the wild creatures.**[8]
>
> ***—President Theodore Roosevelt, at the laying of the Roosevelt Arch cornerstone, 1903***

Visitors can explore the Old Faithful Inn even if they aren't staying there. The hotel's foundations, along with the massive 500-short-ton (454 metric ton) fireplace in its lobby, are made of a dark volcanic rock called rhyolite.[7] Upon entering the hotel, visitors look up to see a soaring structure of natural logs shaped and tied together to form walkways, roof beams, supports, railings, and platforms.

The hotel's interior fixtures, including the chandeliers, dining room chairs, fireplace clock, and front door, are original. For a spectacular view of Old Faithful and the surrounding landscape, visitors can climb to a lookout perch on the building's roof.

While the Old Faithful Inn is impressive, it's not the oldest hotel in the park. That honor belongs to the Lake Yellowstone Hotel, built on the northern shores of the lake in 1891. The Northern Pacific Railway paid for the building's construction. By supporting hotels in the western United States, the railroad company sought to boost passenger traffic along rail routes that crossed the northern Rocky Mountains.

Ghost of the Old Faithful Inn

There are many legends and ghost stories about Yellowstone National Park. One of the most famous stories happened at the Old Faithful Inn. In 1915, a young couple from New York arrived at the hotel. Although they were on their honeymoon, they got into arguments. One night, the husband vanished from the hotel. Days later, hotel maids found the headless body of his murdered bride in the couple's room. A few nights later, while searching the upper floors, staff found the woman's head in the crow's nest. This was a small platform for musicians that loomed over the hotel's lobby. Legend says that ever since the incident, the murdered bride has haunted the Old Faithful Inn.

The lobby of the Old Faithful Inn is 76 feet (23 m) tall. It features original furniture and decorations, including a handmade clock mounted on the stone fireplace.

The Lake Yellowstone Hotel has undergone many changes over the years. In 1903, Robert Reamer designed the Greek columns that rise three stories at the hotel's entrance.[9] In the 1920s, a dining room and sunroom were added to the hotel's first floor. The dining room has large windows that offer a sweeping view of Lake Yellowstone.

Guests can stay at the hotel or in small cabins that were built on the property in the 1920s. Staying at the Lake Yellowstone Hotel or the Old Faithful Inn gives guests a chance to learn about the history of early tourism at the park. Park management wants to keep the historic feel. This means there are no televisions, radios, or air-conditioning units in any of the hotel rooms.

Rustic Places

Yellowstone National Park is also home to three museums, which were built between 1929 and 1932.[10] They are located at Madison, Norris Geyser Basin, and Fishing Bridge. These museums were named National Historic Landmarks in 1987. The buildings were designed to blend in with the park's natural landscape. For that reason, the logs used for the structures were not honed or shaped. They were left as close to their natural state as possible. The same is true of the stone used to build the paths and stairs around the museums.

Historians describe this building style as rustic style or parkitecture. Many buildings in Yellowstone National Park

At the Norris Geyser Basin Museum, visitors can talk to park rangers and see exhibits focused on Yellowstone's geothermal features.

were designed in this way, including the Old Faithful Inn and the Northeast Entrance station and ranger residence. Parkitecture has since caught on as a building style for homes and cabins in many wilderness areas. It inspired buildings in other national parks across the country. When guests arrive at a national park entrance, they may see log structures in dark natural colors that blend in with the landscape.

Keeping human-made structures in tune with the area's natural surroundings has been an important goal for Yellowstone National Park since the early 1900s. But a few modern concessions have been made. To make the park accessible in the winter months, for example, the NPS allows snowcoaches on the roads. There are also boardwalks built around geysers and hot springs to keep curious visitors safe. Yellowstone has even installed webcams in the park so internet users can spot wildlife.

Blending with the Land

Many historians consider Robert Reamer to be the father of parkitecture. As the designer of several famous landmarks, Reamer believed in blending building styles with natural surroundings. He explained that he designed his buildings, including the Old Faithful Inn, out of respect for the land. He said, "I built [the Inn] in keeping with the place where it stands. Nobody could improve upon that. To be at discord with the landscape would be almost a crime. To try to improve upon it would be an impertinence."[11]

CHAPTER
EIGHT

RECREATION IN YELLOWSTONE

Yellowstone National Park offers all kinds of recreational opportunities. Visitors can explore a variety of hiking trails and campsites. They can enjoy watersports at lakes. Many types of outdoor recreation are available at the park year-round.

Yellowstone's network of trails offers hikes for people of all ages and skill levels. Before hiking, guests should spend a day or two acclimating to the area's high elevation. The park sits at an average elevation of about 8,000 feet (2,440 m).[1]

The air is thinner at higher elevations than at lower elevations, so people take in less oxygen with each breath. This can quickly make any physical activity tiring. To prepare, visitors should rest, get enough sleep, and follow a healthy diet.

Fairy Falls is one of Yellowstone National Park's tallest waterfalls. To reach the falls, hikers pass through a scenic lodgepole pine forest.

Hikers who hope to spot wildlife can explore trails in Yellowstone's Lamar Valley. One trail links the valley with Cache Creek. Another trail starts at Fairy Falls and ends at a stretch of geysers and hot springs, including the Imperial and Spray Geysers. Park officials recommend this 6.7-mile (10.8 km) trail for family groups.[2]

Moderate hikes include the climb up Mount Washburn from Dunraven Pass. This trail climbs about 1,400 feet (427 m) over almost seven miles (11.3 km), rewarding hikers with spectacular views of the entire Yellowstone caldera to the west and south.[3] Experienced hikers who are in good shape can also try the Electric Peak and Sky Rim trails, which both run about 20 miles (32 km).[4]

In all, there are about 900 miles (1,450 km) of hiking trails in Yellowstone National Park.[5] Hikers can stop at the park's visitor centers to get maps and trail guides. Visitor center staff can help hikers choose a route and describe current trail conditions. Staff can also inform hikers about

Hiking Fairy Falls

Yellowstone National Park's Fairy Falls Trail is a 4.5-mile (7.2 km) path that takes visitors to a scenic overlook. There's usually not much traffic on this trail because the parking area at the trailhead is small. From the overlook, visitors are rewarded with a view of the colorful Grand Prismatic Spring and Midway Geyser Basin. Along this trail, visitors can also see several geysers. They can see the 200-foot (61 m) Fairy Falls too.[6]

The hike up and down Mount Washburn features a wide trail that winds around the mountain. Hikers on the trail should carry water, bear spray, and snacks with them.

any wolf or bear sightings in the area. To avoid dangerous situations or run-ins with wildlife, it's a good idea to hike in groups of three or more people.

Visitors can also take guided hiking tours. Dozens of local outfitters offer these. Guests learn about the park while hiking. These hikes may last all day or just a few hours.

> **"If you are not very strong, try to climb Electric Peak when a big bossy, well-charged thunder-cloud is on it, to breathe the ozone set free, and get yourself kindly shaken and shocked.[7]**
>
> ***—John Muir, naturalist, in the April 1898 issue of* The Atlantic"**

Camping

Camping is another popular activity in Yellowstone National Park. There are 12 public campgrounds within the park along with more than 2,000 campsites.[8] Before camping at Yellowstone, guests should check the park's website or call a visitor center for current information about weather and trail conditions. The park sometimes closes campgrounds, which means visitors will not be able to get a spot there even if they have reservations.

Backcountry camping is a common way to spend a few days or a single night in Yellowstone. There are 293 campsites along the park's backcountry trails.

Bridge Bay Campground, located near Lake Yellowstone, is one of the largest campgrounds at Yellowstone National Park. Campers at the site can stay in tents or RVs.

The park allows a maximum of three nights at these sites and does not allow overnight camping elsewhere on backcountry trails. A single group of up to 12 people can use a backcountry campsite. The park's rules require campers to obtain a permit. Walk-up permits are available up to two days in advance at the park's backcountry offices, which are located at visitor centers and at ranger stations.[9] Campers can also reserve permits online.

While camping in Yellowstone, visitors must pack and store food with care. Bears and other mammals have an excellent sense of smell and will readily make their way into campsites to forage for food. Yellowstone's backcountry campsites provide poles that visitors can use to hang up their food. Campers must bring their own rope, which must be at least 35 feet (10.7 m) long.[10] This allows people to raise their food to a safe height above the ground, which prevents animals from getting into it.

Some visitors simply want to safely walk around Yellowstone National Park's natural wonders. The park offers 15 miles (24 km) of boardwalks that guide visitors around geothermal features, allowing them to get a close-up look at hot springs, mud pots, fumaroles, and geysers.[11] Guests can also sign up for a range of guided tours, classes, and presentations.

Fishing and Watersports

Yellowstone National Park allows visitors to fish on some of its rivers and lakes. To do so, park guests must obtain a special permit. These permits are valid only in Yellowstone and are available online, at visitor centers, and at ranger stations. Children ages 15 and younger can fish without a permit if they're with an adult.

Park rules protect several native fish species, including cutthroat trout, grayling, and mountain whitefish. Because of this, only catch-and-release fishing of these species is allowed. Non-native species that are caught must be taken out of the park's waterways. These fish must be eaten or thrown away. This is because these species could potentially harm the ecosystem.

The park does not allow fishing at night or fishing by artificial light. The fishing season in Yellowstone National Park runs from late May to October 31. But visitors can fish on the Madison River and Gardner River year-round.

Many guests also enjoy boating at Yellowstone National Park. Visitors can bring their own boats to Yellowstone Lake. However, the park requires sailboats and motorboats to be kept out of the water for at least 30 days before they can be used at the park.[12] Park officials must also inspect boats before they go into

Yellowstone Webcams

The NPS provides a way to see Yellowstone National Park without actually being there in person. Webcams are set up throughout the park. These fixed cameras record footage of the North Entrance, Mammoth Hot Springs, Mount Washburn, the Upper Geyser Basin, and the West Entrance. One webcam positioned at Old Faithful provides a live stream that people can watch on the NPS website. Online visitors can use the park's eruption schedule to tune in to the live streams when geyser eruptions are happening. There's also a webcam that covers traffic conditions at the West Entrance, which is the busiest entrance in the park.

the water. These rules help prevent the introduction of invasive species, such as zebra mussels. All boats are banned from Yellowstone's rivers. However, there is one exception for nonmotorized boats. It is a section of the Lewis River that stretches from Lewis Lake to Shoshone Lake.

Some guests enjoy swimming at Yellowstone National Park. They can do so in the Firehole River along a stretch south of Madison Junction. Due to cold water and strong river currents, the park closes the stream to swimmers until midsummer.

Guided Tours

Some visitors tour Yellowstone National Park on horseback. Outfitters provide horses and experienced guides who know the park's trails. The guides lead groups on day tours or camping trips. Short horseback rides are also offered at Tower-Roosevelt Junction, located at the Northeast Entrance. Here, a horse corral is open for business during the midyear season. The park requires a permit for any people riding their own horses into the park for a day trip.

A few outfitters also offer photography tours and safaris. These guided tours are limited to small groups. Guides check weather forecasts and scout good locations for wildlife along the park's roads or backcountry trails. The group moves around the park in a vehicle that has ample storage for photography equipment.

The guides lead groups to secluded spots where wildlife can be found. In a multiday tour, a photography safari may also visit the park's main attractions. These include Old Faithful, Grand Prismatic Spring, the Lower and Upper Falls, and the Lamar and Hayden Valleys.

From the Air

To get a different perspective of Yellowstone, visitors can arrange an aerial tour. Passengers board a small plane such as a Cessna 182. To avoid disturbing wildlife, planes must stay at least 5,000 feet (1,524 m) above the ground and a half mile (0.8 km) from park boundaries.[13] Aerial tours offer guests a spectacular view of the park's plains and mountain ranges. Other visitors use drones to get a look at hidden or inaccessible places in the mountains. These unmanned aerial vehicles have become a popular way for photographers and filmmakers to get footage. The park requires permits for drones that fly over the park.

On guided snowmobile tours in Yellowstone National Park, guests often stop at geothermal sites and wildlife-watching spots.

Winter Sports

Winters in Yellowstone National Park are often long and harsh. Temperatures drop well below freezing, and a single blizzard can bring several feet of snow. The park closes most roads for the winter season along with several hotels and campgrounds. Only the road that links the North Entrance and Northeast Entrance remains open all year.

However, there are plenty of ways to navigate the park's snowy trails. Cross-country skiing through the Yellowstone wilderness is one of the most popular options. Much of the terrain is flat or slightly hilly, and the area's dry climate makes for fine, powdery snow that's easy to ski on.

Don't Miss It!

The Lower Falls

The Yellowstone River winds its way north from Lake Yellowstone. The river tumbles over a series of white water cascades and two major waterfalls. For many visitors, the highlight of this area is the Lower Falls, a 300-foot (91 m) waterfall at the head of the Grand Canyon of the Yellowstone.[14]

The river carves a steep gorge lined with rocky cliffs, which change color depending on the angle of the sun. These colors are created by a chemical compound called iron oxide. It turns rocks different shades of yellow and orange.

Roads in the vicinity provide access to short trails that lead down into the canyon and along its northern and southern rims. The trails lead hikers to several scenic overlooks, including Lookout Point, Grand View, Artist Point, and Inspiration Point. These overlooks offer spectacular views of the Lower Falls and the river below. Visitors can look out at the same view that inspired painter Thomas Moran during the 1871 Hayden expedition.

Getting around Yellowstone National Park can be tough in the winter. With the roads closed to private cars, the only way to get around is by snowcoach. Snowmobiles are permitted on the main roads but never on the trails. Guests can also reach trailheads by taking a ski shuttle. These are snowcoaches that carry cross-country skiers around the park on a regular schedule. Guided ski tours are also available.

A good base for a winter trip to Yellowstone National Park is West Yellowstone, a small gateway town near the West Entrance. Snowcoaches and guided snowmobile tours depart from this spot. The town also offers sledding, horse-drawn sleigh rides, and ice fishing at nearby Hebgen Lake. Several snowmobile and cross-country ski trails begin in West Yellowstone and lead into the surrounding mountains.

No matter the season, visitors can enjoy countless activities in and around Yellowstone National Park. Nature lovers can trek across the park's many trails, while history buffs can learn about the area's past at museums and historic sites. From wildlife watching to exploring geothermal wonders, Yellowstone offers exciting adventures for the whole family.

ESSENTIAL FACTS

YELLOWSTONE NATIONAL PARK BASICS

- Yellowstone National Park covers 3,472 square miles (8,992 sq km) in northwestern Wyoming, southwestern Montana, and eastern Idaho. It was the first national park in the United States.
- Yellowstone National Park was created by an act of the US Congress that was signed into law by President Ulysses S. Grant in 1872. The National Park Service (NPS) took over management of the park in 1916.
- Yellowstone National Park sits atop a massive underground volcano. It is home to the largest group of geothermal features in the world. Visitors can see geysers, fumaroles, and hot springs.
- Today, Yellowstone National Park is home to 900 miles (1,450 km) of hiking trails, eight National Historic Landmarks, historic hotels, and several museums.

THINGS TO SEE AND DO

- Explore the Upper Geyser Basin and watch the Old Faithful geyser erupt several hundred feet in the air every 90 minutes.
- Go wildlife watching in Lamar Valley to spot wild bison, gray wolves, and other animals.
- Hike to the peak of Mount Washburn to see sweeping views of the Yellowstone caldera.
- Learn about Yellowstone's American Indian history at Obsidian Cliff, the Yellowstone Tribal Heritage Center, or museums throughout the park.
- See the scenic Grand Canyon of the Yellowstone and the Lower Falls of the Yellowstone River.

MAP

QUOTE

"The only way that the people as a whole can secure to themselves and their children the enjoyment in perpetuity of what the Yellowstone Park has to give is by . . . preserving the scenery, the forests, and the wild creatures."

—President Theodore Roosevelt, at the laying of the Roosevelt Arch cornerstone, 1903

GLOSSARY

archaeologist

A person who studies human history by examining artifacts and other physical remains.

cavalry

An army unit of soldiers who fight on horseback.

deciduous

Of or relating to trees that go dormant and shed their leaves in the fall.

fissure

A narrow crack or opening.

geothermal

Of or relating to sources of underground heat.

Global Positioning System (GPS)

A system that uses the timing of signals from orbiting satellites to determine the precise location of a receiver on Earth.

headwaters

The source of a river in smaller streams or in a body of water such as a lake.

invasive species

A species that is introduced to a region where it is not a native inhabitant.

petrified

Turned to stone.

petroglyphs

Designs carved into a rock face or rock wall.

poacher

A hunter who kills animals illegally.

quarry

To mine stone from aboveground deposits.

reservoir

A pool of water collected through natural processes or by artificial means.

resurgent dome

A hill or dome of rock that is slowly rising above the surrounding terrain due to underground volcanic pressure.

stagecoach

A horse-drawn vehicle used to transport passengers and cargo over long distances, using a series of pre-established stops or "stages" for rest and overnight stays.

survey

To map a region and learn more about its geology, soil, flora, and fauna.

ADDITIONAL RESOURCES

SELECTED BIBLIOGRAPHY

Black, George. *Empire of Shadows: The Epic Story of Yellowstone*. St. Martin's, 2012.

Cahill, Tim. *Lost in My Own Backyard: A Walk in Yellowstone National Park*. Crown Journeys, 2004.

St. Louis, Regis. *Yellowstone and Grand Teton National Parks.* Lonely Planet, 2024.

FURTHER READINGS

Lassieur, Allison. *The National Parks Encyclopedia.* Abdo, 2023.

Lomax, Becky. *Best of Yellowstone & Grand Teton.* Moon Travel, 2023.

Storm, Ashley. *Grand Canyon National Park*. Abdo, 2026.

ONLINE RESOURCES

To learn more about Yellowstone National Park, please visit **abdobooklinks.com** or scan this QR code. These links are routinely monitored and updated to provide the most current information available.

MORE INFORMATION

For more information on this subject, contact or visit the following organizations:

NATIONAL PARK SERVICE (NPS)

1849 C St. NW
Washington, DC 20240
nps.gov

The National Park Service (NPS) is a federal agency that manages national parks in the United States, including Yellowstone National Park.

NATIONAL PARKS CONSERVATION ASSOCIATION

777 6th St. NW, Ste. 700
Washington, DC 20001
npca.org

The National Parks Conservation Association is dedicated to protecting US national parks. It keeps track of nearby mining and development projects and their impact on the parks. The organization's volunteers have also helped manage various wildlife.

YELLOWSTONE FOREVER

PO Box 1857
Bozeman, MT 59771
yellowstone.org

Yellowstone Forever is the official nonprofit partner of Yellowstone National Park. The group leads projects to preserve, protect, and enhance the park for visitors. The organization has been involved in wolf research, native fish restoration, a bison tracking and transfer program, and other projects.

SOURCE NOTES

CHAPTER 1. THE HISTORY OF YELLOWSTONE NATIONAL PARK

1. "Hayden and the Founding of the Yellowstone National Park." *US Geological Survey*, 1973, pubs.usgs.gov. Accessed 11 Feb. 2025.

2. "The Four Great Surveys of the West." *US Geological Survey*, 30 Sept. 2019, pubs.usgs.gov. Accessed 11 Feb. 2025.

3. Elizabeth U. Mangan. "Yellowstone, the First National Park." *Library of Congress*, n.d., loc.gov. Accessed 11 Feb. 2025.

4. Ian Webster. "Value of $40,000 from 1870 to 2024." *CPI Inflation Calculator*, n.d., in2013dollars.com. Accessed 11 Feb. 2025.

5. "Colter Stone." *National Park Service*, n.d., nps.gov. Accessed 11 Feb. 2025.

6. "Founding of the Yellowstone National Park."

7. Mangan, "Yellowstone."

8. "Birth of a National Park." *National Park Service*, 5 Feb. 2020, nps.gov. Accessed 11 Feb. 2025.

9. Cole Messa and Ken Sims. "Jim Bridger." *US Geological Survey*, 15 June 2020, usgs.gov. Accessed 11 Feb. 2025.

10. "Explore the Fort Yellowstone Historic District." *National Park Service*, 15 Feb. 2024, nps.gov. Accessed 11 Feb. 2025.

11. "Visitors to Yellowstone National Park from 2008 to 2023." *Statista*, 5 Apr. 2024, statista.com. Accessed 11 Feb. 2025.

12. "Yellowstone Visitors Top 4.6 Million." *Jackson Hole Radio*, 17 Nov. 2024, jacksonholeradio.com. Accessed 11 Feb. 2025.

CHAPTER 2. GETTING THERE AND GETTING AROUND

1. "Facts." *National Park Service*, 4 Apr. 2023, nps.gov. Accessed 11 Feb. 2025.

2. "Bozeman to Yellowstone National Park." *Visit Bozeman*, 26 July 2024, blog.bozemancvb.com. Accessed 11 Feb. 2025.

3. "Yellowstone: Fees & Passes." *National Park Service*, 14 Apr. 2024, nps.gov. Accessed 11 Feb. 2025.

4. "Planning a Trip to Yellowstone National Park." *Roadtrippers*, n.d., roadtrippers.com. Accessed 11 Feb. 2025.

5. "Yellowstone: Visitor Centers." *National Park Service*, 25 Jan. 2022, nps.gov. Accessed 11 Feb. 2025.

6. "Seasonal Closures." *Cody Hotel*, n.d., thecody.com. Accessed 11 Feb. 2025.

7. Gerald R. Ford. "Remarks at Yellowstone." *American Presidency Project*, 29 Aug. 1976, presidency.ucsb.edu. Accessed 11 Feb. 2025.

8. "Old Faithful Inn." *US Park Lodging*, n.d., usparklodging.com. Accessed 11 Feb. 2025.

9. Jayne Clark. "Picnic Spots." *Yellowstone National Park Lodges*, 15 June 2019, yellowstonenationalparklodges.com. Accessed 11 Feb. 2025.

10. Micah Drew. "Second-Highest Visitation Years." *Idaho Capital Sun*, 10 Feb. 2025, idahocapitalsun.com. Accessed 11 Feb. 2025.

CHAPTER 3. EXPLORING YELLOWSTONE'S VOLCANIC HISTORY

1. "Yellowstone Volcano." *Yellowstone National Park Trips*, n.d., yellowstonepark.com. Accessed 12 Feb. 2025.

2. "Facts." *Yellowstone Forever*, n.d., yellowstone.org. Accessed 12 Feb. 2025.

3. Mikaela Ruland. "Upper Geyser Basin." *Yellowstone National Park Trips*, 26 May 2022, yellowstonepark.com. Accessed 12 Feb. 2025.

4. Ruland, "Upper Geyser Basin."

5. "Old Faithful Geyser." *National Park Service*, 9 Dec. 2024, nps.gov. Accessed 12 Feb. 2025.

6. John Clayton. "John Muir in Yellowstone." *WyoHistory*, 6 Aug. 2018, wyohistory.org. Accessed 12 Feb. 2025.

7. Ruland, "Upper Geyser Basin."

8. "Firehole Lake Drive." *Yellowstone National Park Trips*, 3 Mar. 2022, yellowstonepark.com. Accessed 12 Feb. 2025.

9. "Lone Star Geyser Trail." *US News & World Report*, n.d., travel.usnews.com. Accessed 12 Feb. 2025.

10. "Norris Geyser Basin Trails." *National Park Service*, 15 Feb. 2024, nps.gov. Accessed 12 Feb. 2025.

11. "Norris Geyser Basin." *National Park Service*, 25 Nov. 2024, nps.gov. Accessed 12 Feb. 2025.

12. "A Geyser-Gazing Guide to Yellowstone National Park." *Frommer's*, 29 Jan. 2021, frommers.com. Accessed 12 Feb. 2025.

13. Erin Krieger and Mairin Sims. "Yellowstone's Gravest Threat to Visitors." *US Geological Survey*, 31 May 2021, usgs.gov. Accessed 12 Feb. 2025.

CHAPTER 4. YELLOWSTONE'S GEOTHERMAL FEATURES

1. Michael Poland. "Myth about Indigenous People." *Idaho Capital Sun*, 11 Oct. 2023, idahocapitalsun.com. Accessed 12 Feb. 2025.

2. "Fumaroles." *National Park Service*, 18 Apr. 2023, nps.gov. Accessed 12 Feb. 2025.

3. "Yellowstone Supervolcano Revealed." *Yellowstone Forever*, n.d., yellowstone.org. Accessed 12 Feb. 2025.

4. "The Yellowstone Supervolcano." *Yellowstone Treasures*, 3 Aug. 2017, yellowstonetreasures.com. Accessed 12 Feb. 2025.

5. "Secret Places in Yellowstone for an Intimate Experience." *Xanterra Travel Collection*, n.d., xanterra.com. Accessed 12 Feb. 2025.

6. Mark Stelten. "Yellowstone's Most Recent Rhyolite Eruptions." *US Geological Survey*, 23 Oct. 2023, usgs.gov. Accessed 12 Feb. 2025.

7. Stelten, "Yellowstone's Most Recent Rhyolite Eruptions."

SOURCE NOTES CONTINUED

CHAPTER 5. YELLOWSTONE'S FIRST PEOPLES

1. "Yellowstone: Archeology." *National Park Service*, 16 Jan. 2024, nps.gov. Accessed 12 Feb. 2025.

2. Paul Rubinstein. "Native Americans in Yellowstone." *Yellowstone Backcountry Page*, n.d., yellowstonestereoviews.com. Accessed 12 Feb. 2025.

3. Mike Koshmrl. "Movement to 'Re-Indigenize' Yellowstone Gains Steam." *WyoFile*, 13 Sept. 2022, wyofile.com. Accessed 12 Feb. 2025.

4. Richard Grant. "The Lost History of Yellowstone." *Smithsonian Magazine*, Jan. 2021, smithsonianmag.com. Accessed 12 Feb. 2025.

5. "Yellowstone Tribal Heritage Center Opens for Third Season." *Powell Tribune*, 28 May 2024, powelltribune.com. Accessed 12 Feb. 2025.

CHAPTER 6. WILDLIFE IN YELLOWSTONE

1. "Yellowstone National Park Facts." *Yellowstone Forever*, n.d., yellowstone.org. Accessed 12 Feb. 2025.

2. "Fly Fishing the Lamar River." *Montana Angler*, n.d., montanaangler.com. Accessed 12 Feb. 2025.

3. "Bison Ecology." *National Park Service*, 25 Nov. 2024, nps.gov. Accessed 12 Feb. 2025.

4. "Bison Ecology."

5. *Secrets of the National Parks*. 2nd ed., National Geographic, 2020. 182.

6. Brett French. "Lack of Snow Hampers Wolves' Winter Hunting Season." *Spokesman-Review*, 15 May 2024, spokesman.com. Accessed 12 Feb. 2025.

7. "Yellowstone Wolf Project." *Yellowstone Forever*, n.d., yellowstone.org. Accessed 12 Feb. 2025.

8. Matt Cuzzocreo. "Decision Protects Bears." *Greater Yellowstone Coalition*, 8 Jan. 2025, greateryellowstone.org. Accessed 12 Feb. 2025.

9. "Yellowstone Bird Program." *Yellowstone Forever*, n.d., yellowstone.org. Accessed 12 Feb. 2025.

10. "Yellowstone: Safety." *National Park Service*, 7 Aug. 2024, nps.gov. Accessed 12 Feb. 2025.

CHAPTER 7. HISTORIC LANDMARKS

1. Madeline Bilis. "List of All the US National Parks." *Travel + Leisure*, 30 Mar. 2024, travelandleisure.com. Accessed 12 Feb. 2025.

2. "Yellowstone's National Historic Landmarks." *Yellowstone Forever*, n.d., yellowstone.org. Accessed 12 Feb. 2025.

3. Annie Carlson. "The Queen's Laundry." *US Geological Survey*, 18 Apr. 2021, usgs.gov. Accessed 12 Feb. 2025.

4. "Obsidian Cliff." *Scenic Safaris*, n.d., scenic-safaris.com. Accessed 12 Feb. 2025.

5. "Fort Yellowstone." *National Park Service*, 14 Aug. 2023, nps.gov. Accessed 12 Feb. 2025.

6. "Old Faithful Inn." *Yellowstone National Park Trips*, 29 Oct. 2024, yellowstonepark.com. Accessed 12 Feb. 2025.

7. "Old Faithful Inn History." *Yellowstone Forever*, n.d., yellowstone.org. Accessed 12 Feb. 2025.

8. Theodore Roosevelt. "Remarks at Yellowstone National Park." *American Presidency Project*, 24 Apr. 1903, presidency.ucsb.edu. Accessed 12 Feb. 2025.

9. "Renovation of Lake Yellowstone Hotel." *Yellowstone National Park Lodges*, 25 Apr. 2014, yellowstonenationalparklodges.com. Accessed 12 Feb. 2025.

10. "Yellowstone: Trailside Museums." *National Park Service*, 14 Aug. 2023, nps.gov. Accessed 12 Feb. 2025.

11. Lauren Harrison. "'Parkitecture' in Yellowstone." *US Geological Survey*, 23 May 2022, usgs.gov. Accessed 12 Feb. 2025.

CHAPTER 8. RECREATION IN YELLOWSTONE

1. Stephen Camelio. "Yellowstone's Mountain Tops." *Yellowstone Forever*, 9 Sept. 2019, yellowstone.org. Accessed 12 Feb. 2025.

2. "Fairy Falls to Imperial Geyser." *Yellowstone Forever*, n.d., yellowstone.org. Accessed 12 Feb. 2025.

3. "Mount Washburn Trail." *Wildland Trekking*, 21 Feb. 2019, wildlandtrekking.com. Accessed 12 Feb. 2025.

4. Ebony Roberts. "Hikes." *57hours*, n.d., 57hours.com. Accessed 12 Feb. 2025.

5. "Yellowstone: Hike a Trail." *National Park Service*, 18 July 2024, nps.gov. Accessed 12 Feb. 2025.

6. "Fairy Falls Trailhead." *National Park Service*, 19 Nov. 2024, nps.gov. Accessed 12 Feb. 2025.

7. John Clayton. "John Muir in Yellowstone." *WyoHistory*, 6 Aug. 2018, wyohistory.org. Accessed 12 Feb. 2025.

8. "FAQ." *Yellowstone Forever*, n.d., yellowstone.org. Accessed 12 Feb. 2025.

9. "Camp in the Backcountry." *National Park Service*, 13 Jan. 2025, nps.gov. Accessed 12 Feb. 2025.

10. "Camp in the Backcountry."

11. "Trails." *Yellowstone Forever*, n.d., yellowstone.org. Accessed 12 Feb. 2025.

12. "Yellowstone: Boat on a Lake." *National Park Service*, 16 Jan. 2025, nps.gov. Accessed 12 Feb. 2025.

13. "New FAA Rules for Flying over National Parks." *Cunningham Swaim*, 18 Mar. 2024, cunninghamswaim.com. Accessed 12 Feb. 2025.

14. "Grand Canyon of the Yellowstone." *National Park Service*, 15 Feb. 2024, nps.gov. Accessed 12 Feb. 2025.

INDEX

ABOUT THE AUTHOR

TOM STREISSGUTH

Tom Streissguth has been writing nonfiction and reference books for schools and libraries for more than 30 years. His interests include music, movies, travel, food, and all kinds of books, including mysteries, history books, biographies, and the works of international authors such as Milan Kundera, Yukio Mishima, Martin Amis, and Naguib Mahfouz. He founded The Archive, an online collection of historic journalism by American authors, which has gathered more than 10,000 rare and interesting pieces. He lives in the Twin Cities area, where he grew up, and has three daughters.